W9-CHR-632

101

Things To Do In

DOOR

COUNTY

By Richard Rusnack II

Copyright 1996
Avery Color Studios, Inc.

Library of Congress Card No. 96-084994
ISBN 0-932212-91-3
First Edition – 1996
Revised Edition — 1996, 2000

Published by Avery Color Studios, Inc.
Gwinn, Michigan 49841

Proudly printed in Michigan, U.S.A.

Introduction

This little collection of ideas began as a simple itinerary I created for a guest who asked me to map out a full weekend of things to do in Door County. It seemed like such a perfect way to keep my guests happy and busy during their visits that I started a little journal of things to do, and continued adding to it for years. That tattered old journal, which started as just a few reminders, has somehow made it onto the pages of this little book.

This is a very personal listing of suggestions I've shared over the years with family and friends. Some businesses are mentioned but this is not meant to be an advertisement, these are places which have stood the test of time and have long been family favorites.

I hope you will use this book in much the same way I have; consider it a puzzle that can be assembled a thousand different ways; choose at random and build a day, a week, a summer, just use your imagination, and the key to the Door is yours.

Enjoy the County!

> *"ILLE TERRARUM MIHI PRAETER
> OMNIS ANGULUS RIDET"*
>
> ~Horace Odes 2, 6, 13-14

Translation:
This little corner of the earth to me smiles
beyond all others.

In Memory of
Deanne Graf

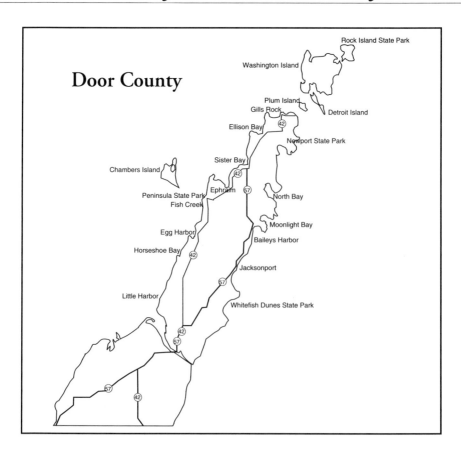

Door County

Rock Island State Park

Washington Island

Plum Island
Gills Rock
Detroit Island
Ellison Bay
42
Newport State Park

Sister Bay
Chambers Island
42
Ephraim
57
Peninsula State Park
North Bay
Fish Creek

Moonlight Bay
Egg Harbor
Baileys Harbor
Horseshoe Bay
42
Jacksonport
57
Little Harbor
Whitefish Dunes State Park
42
57

57
42

• 1 •

Rent a kayak or paddleboat
at Fish Creek Harbor,
paddle up Fish Creek,
when you see the Viking
boat, beach your craft and
splurge on a frozen custard
at the creek-side stand.

•2•

Turn your day into a treasure hunt for the hidden lakes of Door County: Little, Europe, Mud, Kangaroo, Mackaysee, Lost, Clark, Arber, Schwartz & Dunes. You can pick up a detailed local map at most hardware stores and filling stations.

•3•

*Go ballroom dancing
at the Alpine
Resort's spring
Blossom Ball.*

•4•

Don't miss Door
County's largest parade:
the Blossom Parade in
Egg Harbor, May.

•5•

Take the car ferry across to Washington Island to visit the Jacobsen Indian Museum. If you have plenty of time and a beautiful day, take your bikes, if not, a car is a must.

•6•

Visit the monument in
Ephraim which
commemorates the landing
of the Moravians in 1853.
The monument is even
more interesting if you
stop first at Wilson's for
an ice cream.

•7•

Call ahead to reserve a pallet of strawberries at Schartner's Farm Market, once you've tried them you'll understand why you need a reservation. They are located a few miles south of Egg Harbor on Hwy. 42.

•8•

Catch a local favorite: the talent show on the Friday night that kicks off "Olde Ellison Bay Days" weekend in July. The show is held in the Ellison Bay Firehouse, just off of Hwy. 42 on Garrett Bay Road.

•9•

Find the original cabin of Asa Thorpe, one of Door County's earliest settlers, and founder of Fish Creek. The old log home is just out the back door of The Silly Goose shop at Founder's Square.

•10•

Take a trip back in time, visit the Pioneer Schoolhouse on Moravia St. in Ephraim.

•11•

Attend a concert at the Birch Creek Music Center in Egg Harbor. To make it a complete, wonderful evening have dinner before hand at Trio, also in Egg Harbor.

•12•

See a performance at the
American Folklore Theatre
in Peninsula State Park.
This is a rustic open-air
theatre, so bring a blanket
and some bug spray. The
show makes a perfect finale
to a day of hiking, biking or
sunning in the park.

•13•

Pick up some great home decorating ideas at the annual House and Garden Walk in Sister Bay; to benefit Door County Memorial Hospital.

• 14 •

Don't miss the locally famous Door County Antique Show in Fish Creek at Gibraltar High School in July.

•15•

*Take a class at the
Peninsula Art School in
Fish Creek.*

•16•

If you're willing to be a
little more adventurous, do
some scuba diving. Much of
Door County's early
mystique came from its
reputation for treacherous
waters (e.g. "Death's
Door"). The many wrecks
in our surrounding waters
substantiate the lore.

•17•

Try to golf all <u>27</u> holes
at the Alpine Resort
course in Egg Harbor.
Call ahead for a tee
time, this is one of the
county's busiest courses.

•18•

Have breakfast at the
Village Cafe in Egg
Harbor. Then pick up
fixings for a picnic lunch
and drive south on County
G for a day at the beach
in Murphy Park.

•19•

Have a true "Door County" breakfast…Door County berry-sour cream coffee cake at the White Gull Inn in Fish Creek; then take a long, and much needed walk down Cottage Row.

•20•

Go downhill skiing or
snowboarding on the lift
serviced hill at
Potawatomi State Park.

•21•

You'll find lots of fish boils in Door County; go to the one that started it all - The Viking Restaurant in Ellison Bay, home of the original fish boil. Three miles north of Sister Bay on Hwy. 42.

• 22 •

Spend an evening at
Peninsula Players. This
water front, open-air
theatre provides the setting
for a perfect night out.
Arrive early with a picnic,
then stroll the grounds and
soak-up the sunset before
curtain call.

•23•

Go to Cave Point on a stormy day to watch the waves crash against the cliffs. The park access is south of Jacksonport on Hwy. 57.

• 24 •

Pick up a couple sandwiches at the Fish Creek General Store, walk to the Fish Creek entrance to Peninsula State Park, hike to Welker's Point. Enjoy the view over lunch.

•25•

Join the Polar Bear
Club. Meet at the
Jacksonport Park in
January. Initiation is
simple: just jump into
the frozen lake, if you
survive, you're a new
member!

•26•

Explore your palette when you order wine by the flight at Sage on 3rd Avenue in Sturgeon Bay. Sage wins my family's vote for best "special occasion" dining in Door County; innovative menu, attentive service and a warm, sophisticated atmosphere.

•27•

Rent a Jet Ski in Ephraim and thrash the waves of Eagle Harbor.

•28•

If you're a thrill seeker who enjoys the wind in your hair, try parasailing over Eagle Harbor, Ephraim.

•29•

The standards are low, but the games are fun at the Fish Creek Winter Games, February.

• 30 •

Join the Wildflower
Pilgrimage event at the
Ridges Sanctuary in May,
Baileys Harbor.

•31•

The whistle blows, the conductor bellows, "Fish Creek, next stop" as your lunch chugs towards you on the flat-bed car of a toy train. The kids are going to love this! P.C. Junction, at the corner of A and E due east of Egg Harbor.

•32•

Take a guided kayak tour of the Mink River Estuary; only reachable by boat, it remains one of Door County's most pristine and secluded wilderness areas. Call Bayshore Outdoor in Sister Bay to plan your trip.

•33•

Eat out Wisconsin style at The Mill Supper Club on Hwy. 42 in Sturgeon Bay. Have your drinks and order from the bar, your waitress will seat you when your dinner is served.

•34•

Just north of Ellison Bay on Hwy. 42 there is a little sign which reads "NP." This is the road to Newport State Park. The hiking trails along Lake Michigan north of the third parking lot are my favorite in the county.

•35•

Dedicate a day to the arts, stop in every art gallery you see.

•36•

Grab your favorite lawn chairs and take in a "Concert in the Park" on Wednesday afternoons at 3:00 pm at the Sister Bay Village park.

•37•

Run or walk the Hairpin
5K Race in Fish Creek the
morning of the 4th of July.
The race starts in the bank
parking lot and finishes
behind Founder's Square.
This is a great way to start
a memorable family day;
for many, it has
become a tradition.

• 38 •

Don't miss "The Tasting Table" inside The Silly Goose General Store. They sample dozens of Door County specialty foods every day. Located both in Fish Creek and Ellison Bay.

•39•

Watch the firemen battle for top honors at the Gibraltar Fisherman's Festival. The competition is held at Clark Park in Fish Creek.

•40•

Catch a glimpse of local life at the Door County Fair in August. The fair grounds are located just west of Hwy. 42 in Sturgeon Bay.

•41•

Visit the most unique Door County gallery I've found: Edgewood Orchards, south of Fish Creek just off of Hwy. 42 on Peninsula Players Road.

•42•

One of my fondest memories as a child in Door County is cooking out in the winter time. Get the family bundled up and head to Peninsula, Newport or Whitefish Dunes State Park, all have grills and picnic tables available for 4-season cookouts.

•43•

Wait for the perfect evening, then enjoy a little romance on the Sunset Concert Cruise. You can find their brochure at any visitor's office.

• 44 •

Stop by and say hello to one of Door County's original artisans at the Potter's Wheel, across from Gibraltar High School in Fish Creek.

•45•

Don't miss Egg Harbor's Pumpkin Patch Festival in early October. It's one of the county's best.

•46•

Take a walk down historic Third Ave. in Sturgeon Bay, have lunch at either Perry's Cherry Diner, or The Inn at Cedar Crossing.

•47•

Kick off your visit to
the county with a bag
of fresh cheese curds
from Renard's cheese
factory, located on both
Hwys. "S" and "57."
Ask for the curds so
fresh they squeak.

•48•

Spend a day on horseback
at one of the many local
riding stables.

•49•

Get a bird's eye view of the county - charter a sight-seeing plane out of Ephraim's municipal airport.

•50•

You must do this at least once in a lifetime: ski by candlelight through one of Door County's State Parks. Wait until you are deep into the woods, then stop and listen to the sound of winter. On a cold, calm night you can almost hear the beat of your own heart. Call the park office for dates and locations.

•51•

Take your sweetheart to "Champagne Rock." Park in Fish Creek, then walk south on Cottage Row until you reach the base of Hairpin Curve. There is a sliver of land roughly 30' x 200', it is a public park. Down at the water's edge there is a rock ledge which hangs out over the crashing waves. This wonderful little spot is known as Champagne Rock.

•52•

Ride or hike the Ahnapee State trail from Sturgeon Bay to Algoma.

•53•

Follow the annual Door County Lighthouse Walk, sponsored by the Door County Maritime Museum in mid-May (920-743-9598). The self-guided tour will take you in or around many of the mainland lighthouses. Boat tours are available to reach the more isolated island lighthouses.

•54•

On your way into northern Door County stop at the Door County Museum (18 N. 4th Ave., Sturgeon Bay) you'll see one of the most spectacular wildlife exhibits in the state. This painstakingly created, hand painted display of our native species is just the beginning of the complete story of Door County.

•55•

All new, but guaranteed to stand the test of time. Horseshoe Bay Farms Golf Course and Clubhouse set a new standard of excellence for the Door County golf experience.

•56•

Applaud a sunset from Ellison Bay Bluff park. It is the best performance in the county. Take Hwy. 42 three miles north of Sister Bay, turn left at the (small) Ellison Bay Bluff park sign.

•57•

After you visit Ellison Bay Bluff park, you might want to stop for lunch and a little shopping in the town of Ellison Bay; this quiet little local's haven still reminds me of the Door County I came to 20 years ago.

•58•

Hop in the car, find your favorite orchard and pick your own cherries, apples, strawberries, raspberries… etc.

•59•

There are few places left in the world where French toast for breakfast means first baking the bread from scratch. You'll find this kind of attention to detail when you stay at the Inn on Maple in Sister Bay.

•60•

See the Bjorklunden Chapel. It is one of the county's most charming and historically interesting landmarks. You can find a map with complete directions in any town's visitor's office.

•61•

Grab a burger at the bar of
Casey's Inn, Egg Harbor.
It's one of the town's oldest
restaurants and has a
fantastic view of the bay.

•62•

One of my favorite finishes to a long day of work or play in Door County is a margarita (or two) at La Puerta at the north end of Sister Bay. Keep the made-from-scratch chips and salsa coming!

•63•

Bake a Door County Cherry Pie.

~Pastry for a 2-crust 9" pie.

~6 cups frozen Door County cherries or 2~16 oz. cans water-packed Door County Cherries, drained. You can find either of these at most of Door County's farm stands.

~3 tablespoons tapioca (quick-cooking.)

~1-1/3 cups sugar.

~1/4 teaspoon almond extract.

Combine fruit, tapioca, sugar and extract in bowl; let stand 15 minutes. Fill pastry shell with fruit mixture; dot with one tablespoon butter or margarine. Add top crust; seal and flute edges. Cut slits in top pastry to allow steam to escape. Bake at 400 degrees for 65-70 minutes. Serve warm with vanilla ice cream.

•64•

Support the Door County Land Trust in their efforts to protect and preserve Door County's open spaces through conservation easements and land donations. The group maintains informational displays inside the Silly Goose General Stores in Fish Creek and Ellison Bay.

• 65 •

Experience the Door
County coastline from a
kayak. Rent one for the day
at the boat launch in Fish
Creek or Nicolet Beach in
Peninsula State Park.

•66•

Explore a little WW2 history right here in Door County. During the summer of 1945, a German POW camp was set up on land which is now part of Peninsula State Park in Fish Creek. Ask a ranger to point it out on a map and see if you can find any signs of the old camp. The POWs spent much of their time picking cherries, as most of our men had been shipped over-seas.

•67•

I can't think of a better way to
start a Sunday morning than
with a fresh baked croissant
and a world-class cup of coffee
at Leroy's in Ephraim. A great
place to linger over your copy
of the Journal or New York
Times while planning your slow
attack on the day.

•68•

Take a walk with the
Gibraltar Historical
Association. Historical
Walks of Old Fish Creek
depart weekly from the
Gibraltar Town Hall
(located in Fish Creek).

•69•

As a local, my favorite place to play tourist is out on the waters of Eagle Harbor in Ephraim. Treat yourself to a cooler full of local specialty foods and beverages, rent one of those silly pontoon boats, then cruise on over to Nicolet Bay to join the flotilla of yachts. What better way to relax than on your own private island!

•70•

On the summer solstice head to Ephraim just before sunset to see the burning of the winter witch. Every year the Scandinavian Fyr Ball Festival welcomes the beginning of summer by setting symbolic bonfires around the perimeter of Eagle Harbor and crowning a Fyr Ball Chieftain.

•71•

Take a guided tour of the
Sturgeon Bay shipyards.
Call the Sturgeon Bay
Rotary Club for info.

•72•

Go to a drive-in movie in Fish Creek. Take lots of blankets and pillows and sit under the stars on the lawn up front. Save room for snacks, the concessions even offer foot-longs and pizza!

•73•

Tried & True
for Lunch:

P.C. Junction

Diggers

Perry's Cherry Diner

The Cookery

Johnny G's Deli

•74•

Enjoy some of the county's best biking roads just north of Ellison Bay and west of Hwy. 42. Take a left at Gus Klenke's Garage to bike along the shoreline all the way from Ellison Bay to Gill's Rock.

•75•

Tried & True
for Dinner:

Sage
T. Ashwell's
Sister Bay Bowl
Hotel du Nord
The Mission Grill
Trio
The Shoreline
Bayou on 3rd
Inn at Kristoffer's

•76•

*Take the moonlight
cruise to Rock Island.*

•77•

Drive by the most beautiful farm in all of Door County: Horseshoe Bay Farm, south of Egg Harbor on County G.

•78•

Have a cookout at
Murphy Park. Go in late
afternoon or early
evening so you don't
miss the spectacular
sunset view.
Follow County G three
miles south of Egg Harbor.

•79•

Tried & True
for Breakfast:

Pelletier's Patio at Founder's Square
Carroll House
Al Johnson's
The White Gull Inn
T. Ashwells Sunday brunch

•80•

Visit the newly restored Noble Historic House on the corner of Main and Hwy. 42 in downtown Fish Creek. One of the oldest original buildings in town, the restoration and lifestyle decorations offer a wonderful insight into life in Door County near the turn of the century.

•81•

Visit the Cana Island Lighthouse.

Follow Hwy. 57 north; turn right on County Q.

•82•

Ask a local where his favorite "spot" is to just sit and soak up the scenery. I guarantee you'll be led to a beautiful and different place every time.

•83•

Visit the Door County
Historical Museum in
Sturgeon Bay on the
morning of your first day.
It will enrich your
whole vacation.

•84•

Indulge at Wilson's Ice
Cream Parlor in
Ephraim.
Often.

•85•

Bowl a few lines at the Sister Bay Bowl. You might want to stay for dinner; they have the best perch in the county.

•86•

Visit the Pioneer store in
Ellison Bay. It's a step
back in time; the store is
still heated in the winter
by an antique wood stove.

•87•

Tried & True Lodging:

Inn on Maple
Juniper Inn
White Gull Inn
Whistling Swan
Ephraim Inn
Hotel du Nord

• 88 •

Play in the sand dunes at Whitefish Dunes State Park. You'll find the park entrance south of Baileys Harbor on Hwy. 57.

•89•

Go to Schoolhouse Beach
on Washington Island at
sunset; if you're looking
for romance, you'll be
swept away.

•90•

Drive to the Anderson dock at the north end of Ephraim on Hwy. 42, walk down to the old barn and read the "antique" graffiti.

•91•

Go for a drive by a different set of rules: you can go anywhere you like without using Hwys. 42 or 57. Don't be afraid to get lost, you'll never be more than 30 minutes from home, unless you swim.

•92•

Investigate the continuing
education courses at "The
Clearing" in Ellison Bay.
Plan your next trip around
a seminar or class.

•93•

Take a walk down Garrett
Bay Road in Ellison Bay.
Walk all the way to the
boat launch, this is one
of my favorite little
"spots" in Door County.

•94•

Drive or bike from
Ephraim to Ellison Bay
on "Olde Stage Road,"
this main street provides
access to northern Door's
least travelled and most
scenic country roads.

•95•

Visit the Great Hall on Rock Island.

•96•

Going to <u>The Farm</u> is a
must. I've been to this
petting zoo a dozen times
and I love it more with
every visit. Just north of
Sturgeon Bay on Hwy. 57.

•97•

Enjoy some of the county's best bird-watching at the Ridges Sanctuary in Baileys Harbor.

•98•

Tried & True
Bars & Nightlife:

The Shoreline (at sunset)
Bayside Tavern
AC Tap
La Puerta
Peninsula Pub
C&C Club

•99•

Learn a little nautical
history at the Door
County Maritime Museum
in Gills Rock.

•100•

Go to Al Johnson's restaurant to see the goats on the grass roof of the authentic Swedish building. Take a picture with the goats behind you in the distance so that it appears a tiny goat is standing on your head!

• 101 •

Rent a few snowmobiles,
bundle up, and explore
the endless miles of
trails throughout the
county. You'll find some
of the best riding in
Peninsula State Park.

For more information about Door County, call:

24-hour Fishing Hotline	(920) 743-7046
Sturgeon Bay Weather	(920) 743-6577
Door County Chamber of Commerce	(920) 743-4456
Fish Creek Information	(920) 868-2316
Egg Harbor Information	(920) 868-3717
Ephraim Information	(920) 854-4989
Sister Bay Information	(920) 854-2812
Ellison Bay Information	(920) 854-5448
Bailey's Harbor Information	(920) 839-2366

Door County Parks:

Peninsula State Park
Box 218
Fish Creek WI 54212
(920) 868-3258

Newport State Park
(Backpack campsites only)
475 County Hwy. NP
Ellison Bay WI 54210
(920) 854-2500

Whitefish Dunes State Park
3701 Clark Lake Road
Sturgeon Bay WI 54235
(920) 823-2400

Potowatomi State Park
3740 Park Drive
Sturgeon Bay WI 54235
(920) 743-8869

Rock Island State Park
Washington Island WI
54246
(920) 743-8869

Ahnapee State Trail
Sturgeon Bay WI 54235
(920) 743-5123

~Dear Reader~

If you have discovered a certain special something or place in Door County, and would like to pass it along, please write it down and send it to me. I would welcome the chance to share it with other readers in a future book.

Thanks!

Richard Rusnack II
P.O. Box 500
Sister Bay, WI 54234

~My special thing to do in Door County~

~My special thing to do in Door County~

~My special thing to do in Door County~

About the Author

Richard Rusnack II received his B.A. in English and French Literature from Colby College in Waterville, Maine. He lives in Ellison Bay, Wisconsin, where he is President of The Silly Goose General Stores, a family business, established in Fish Creek in 1969.

Look for *101 Grand Adventures In Traverse City* by Richard Rusnack II, also by Avery Color Studios, Inc.

Avery Color Studios, Inc. has a full line of Great Lakes oriented books, cookbooks, puzzles, shipwreck and lighthouse maps, and lighthouse posters.

For a full color catalog call:
1-800-722-9925